ROYAL COURT

✖ Ulster Bank
DUBLIN THEATRE FESTIVAL

Royal Court Theatre, Ulster Bank Dublin Theatre Festival and Pentabus Theatre Company present

KEBAB

by **Gianina Carbunariu**

translated by **Philip Osment**

First performance at Ulster Bank Dublin Theatre Festival,
Project Cube, Dublin, 27 September 2007.

First performance at Royal Court Theatre, Jerwood Theatre Upstairs,
Sloane Square, London on 19 October 2007.

KEBAB is presented as part of International Playwrights Season: A Genesis Project,
with additional support from the Romanian Cultural Institute, London.

Media Partner
THE ✖ INDEPENDENT

Genesis
FOUNDATION

KEBAB

by **Gianina Carbunariu**
translated by **Philip Osment**

Bogdan **Sam Crane**
Madalina **Matti Houghton**
Voicu **Laurence Spellman**

Director **Orla O'Loughlin**
Designer **Simon Daw**
Lighting Designer **Philip Gladwell**
Sound Designer **Neil Alexander**
Assistant Director **Kat Joyce**
Casting Director **Amy Ball**
Production Manager **Sue Bird**
Stage Managers **Carla Archer, Bryony Milne**
Dialect Coach **Anne Walsh**
Costume Supervisor **Jackie Orton**

With special thanks to the following for their help with the development of this play:
The British Council, Cristina Catalina, Sean Holmes, John London, The Ratiu Foundation,
Graham Whybrow, Tom Wilson.

The Royal Court and Stage Management wish to thank the following for their help with this
production: Canon, Jap Auto Parts, Polaroid.

THE COMPANY

Gianina Carbunariu (writer)
Gianina is a director and a playwright. She is one of the directors for dramAcum project, which specialises in contemporary drama in Romania. Kebab has been staged in Munich Kammerspiele Theater, Schaubuhne in Berlin, and Theater Studio d'Alfortville in Paris. Kebab has also been translated into Russian, Italian, Greek, Polish, Czech and Slovak. The first production of Kebab, performed under the title mady-baby.edu, was staged in Foarte Mic Theatre in Bucharest directed by Gianina. It went on to participate in festivals in France, Slovakia, Germany, Russia and Poland.
Other plays include: Stop the Tempo (Germany/France/Ireland); DJ Pirat (France); All These Guys Look like Our Parents (Tristan Bates); Unrealities from the Immediate Wild East.

Neil Alexander (sound designer)
For the Royal Court: On Tour (with Liverpool Everyman), The Lying Kind, Yard Gal, Been So Long, Fair Game, Bailegangaire, Heredity, Penetrator.
Other theatre includes: Maps (National Studio); The Night Season, Democracy, Power, Elmina's Kitchen, Honour, A Prayer for Owen Meany, Life After Life, Vincent in Brixton, Mother Clap's Molly House, Marriage Play, Finding the Sun, Remembrance of Things Past, The Waiting Room, Blue/Orange, Sparkleshark (National); She Stoops To Conquer, A Laughing Matter (Out Of Joint/National); Big Love, The Arab Israeli Cookbook, Two Horsemen (Gate); Amadeus (Wilton's Music Hall); Animal Farm (Derby Playhouse); The Long & The Short & The Tall, The Little Fir Tree, Macbeth (Crucible); The Charge of the Light Brigade (Complicite Workshop); Vanishing Points (Complicite); The Rubenstein Kiss, Jeffrey Dahmer Is Unwell (Hampstead); The Laramie Project, Frankie & Johnny (Sound); The Lemon Princess (West Yorkshire Playhouse); The Slab Boys, Cutting a Rug, Still Life (Traverse); Observe the Sons of Ulster Marching Towards the Somme, Normal – The Dusseldorf Ripper (Pleasance); Biloxi Blues (New Vanburgh); Private Dancer (Brighton Art College); The Snake House (Greenwich Studio); The Year of the Family (Finborough).
Neil is Deputy Sound & IT Lecturer at Guildhall School of Music & Drama.

Sam Crane
Theatre includes: Othello (Globe); Ghosts (Bristol Old Vic); Carrie's War (Lilian Bayliss); Midnight Cowboy (Assembly Rooms, Edinburgh); Silverland (Arcola); And Then There Were None (Gielgud); 24 Hour Plays (Old Vic); Ubu Roi (Young Vic); Major Barbara (Manchester Royal Exchange); Rabbit (Frantic Assembly); A Little Requiem for Kantor (ICA/Sesc Sao Paulo).
Television includes: Midsomer Murders, The Sins, Doctors.
Radio includes: The Pretenders, Shadowbaby.
Sam trained at LAMDA.

Simon Daw (designer)
For the Royal Court: Young Writers Festival 2002.
Other theatre includes: The Enchantment (National); Elling (Trafalgar Studios/Bush); French Without Tears (English Touring Theatre); Not The Love I Cry For (Arcola); Aladdin (Bristol Old Vic); Jackets (Young Vic/Theatre 503); The Bodies (Live Theatre); Rutherford and Son (Royal Exchange); Tall Phoenix (Belgrade); Romeo and Juliet (RSC); Adam and Eve (TPT, Tokyo); Astronaut (Theatre O/Barbican Pit/tour); The Changeling (National Studio); Rafts and Dreams, Across Oka (Royal Exchange Studio); Relatively Speaking, The Witches, Everyman, Habeas Corpus (Northampton); Under the Curse, Tragedy: A Tragedy (Gate); Touched (RSAMD); The Singing Group, Exclude Me (Chelsea Theatre); Fragile Land (Hampstead); The Arbitrary Adventures of an Accidental Terrorist (NYT/Lyric Hammersmith Studio); Kes (NYT/Lyric Hammersmith).
Dance includes: Bloom (Rambert); The Stepfather (CandoCo Dance Co.).
Opera includes: Fidelio (Scottish Opera).
Installation & performance commissions include: Wavestructures (Aldeburgh Festival/online); Hopefully It Means Nothing (Aldeburgh Festival/National); New Town (site specific/Arches Glasgow); Sea House (Aldeburgh Festival).

Philip Gladwell (lighting designer)
Theatre includes: The Member of the Wedding, Winners, Interior, The Exception and the Rule, The New Tennant, When the World was Green, The Soul of Ch'ien Nu Leaves Her Body, Action, Streetcar to Tennessee (Young Vic); Terminus (Abbey, Dublin); Melody, In the Bag (Traverse); Midnight Cowboy (Assembly); A Whistle in the Dark (Citizens); HOTBOI, Tape (Soho); Jack and the Beanstalk, Aladdin (Hackney Empire); Dead Funny, Mother Courage (Nottingham Playhouse/UK tour); Into the Woods, Macbeth, Way Up Stream (Derby Playhouse); Jackets (Theatre 503/Young Vic); The Bodies (Live Theatre); The Morris (Liverpool Everyman); Bread & Butter (Tricycle); Mixed Feelings (UK tour); Sophie Tucker's One Night Stand (King's Head/New End); Paper Thin (Kali Theatre Co. tour); Finders Keepers (Theatre Rites); Dreams From a Summer House (Watermill); The Tempest (National); Modern Love (Queen Elizabeth Hall); Unite for the Future (Old Vic).

Opera includes: Cavalleria Rusticana, Pagliacci (Haddo House Opera); Another America: Fire (Sadler's Wells); An Operatic Evening (ROH). Ballet includes: The Canterville Ghost (Peacock); Awakening (Sadler's Wells).

Matti Houghton
For the Royal Court: International Residency Presentations 2007.
Other theatre includes: Kindertransport (Shared Experience); Watership Down (Lyric Hammersmith); Burn, Chatroom, Citizenship, The Menu (National); Stallerhof (Southwark Playhouse); Mikey the Pikey (Pleasance, Edinburgh). Television includes: Afterlife II, The Last Detective. Matti trained at Guildhall School of Music & Drama.

Kat Joyce (assistant director)
For the Royal Court: Open House Street Theatre 2007 (co-directed with Ola Animashawun).
As director, other theatre includes:
A Man Somewhere/A Woman Somewhere Else (Back Hill Studios); The Veiled Conspiracy (Sala Impermiable, Seville/International Drama Festival, Bilbao); R&C (Sala Endanza, Seville).
As assistant director, other theatre includes: Game? (Tangled Feet, Theatre 503/Gilded Balloon, Edinburgh); Underground (Dreamthinkspeak, Brighton Theatre Royal/barbicanbite05/Young Vic).
Kat is co-founder of Sour Feast Theatre Co.

Orla O'Loughlin (director)
For the Royal Court: Small Talk: Big Picture, Angry Now, No Farewell, … of the Cities.
Other theatre includes: How Much is Your Iron? (Young Vic); The Hound of the Baskervilles (tour/West End); The Fire Raisers, Sob Stories, Refrain, Go the Way Your Blood Beats, Norman (BAC); A Dulditch Angel (tour); Lorca: The Playwright, Lorca: The Poet (National); Vienna Dreaming, Sam and Lucy, Let Your Heart Break Open, Maps, The Mum Project (National Theatre Studio);

Redemption (New Dramatists, New York).
Awards include: James Menzies-Kitchin Director's Award; Carlton Bursary at the Donmar Warehouse.
Formerly International Associate at the Royal Court, Orla is now Artistic Director of Pentabus Theatre Company.

Philip Osment (translator)
Translations and adaptations include: Pedro the Great Pretender (RSC); Duck! (Unicorn).
Other plays include: Telling Tales, This Island's Mine, The Undertaking (Gay Sweatshop); Who's Breaking?, Sleeping Dogs (Red Ladder); Listen (Theatre Centre); The Dearly Beloved, What I Did in the Holidays, Flesh and Blood, Buried Alive (Method and Madness); Wise Guys (Theatre Centre/Red Ladder); Little Violet and the Angel (Theatre Centre/Macrobert Theatre Stirling); Leaving (Quare Hawks, Ireland); Collateral Damage (LAMDA); A Happy Release (Theatre Royal, Plymouth); Palace of Fear (Leicester Haymarket).
Radio plays include: The Last Resort, Little Violet, Maurice.
Awards include: Writers' Guild Best Regional Play Award 1993 for The Dearly Beloved; co-winner of the Peggy Ramsey Award 2000 for Little Violet and the Angel.
Philip learned Romanian during the three years that he was dramaturg and director of With Love from Nikolae (Clear Day with Teatrul Dramatic, Constanta/Bristol Old Vic).

Laurence Spellman
Theatre includes: Cymbeline (Cheek by Jowl, Barbican/International tour); Bent (Trafalgar Studios); The Changeling (Cheek by Jowl, Barbican/European tour); Antony and Cleopatra (Manchester Royal Exchange); Charley's Aunt (Northcott Exeter); They Shoot Horses Don't They? (NYT/West End).
Television includes: The Waltz King.
Film includes: The Libertine, Stage Fright.

THE ENGLISH STAGE COMPANY AT THE ROYAL COURT

'For me the theatre is really a religion or way of life. You must decide what you feel the world is about and what you want to say about it, so that everything in the theatre you work in is saying the same thing ... A theatre must have a recognisable attitude. It will have one, whether you like it or not.'

George Devine, first artistic director of the English Stage Company: notes for an unwritten book.

The Royal Court Theatre in London's Sloane Square has presented some of the most influential plays in modern theatre history. At the turn of the twentieth century, the Royal Court was under the direction of Harley Granville-Barker and staged plays by Ibsen, Galsworthy, Yeats, Maeterlinck and Shaw. In 1956 George Devine became the first Artistic Director of the English Stage Company at the Royal Court. His intention was to create an international theatre of experiment that was devoted to the discovery of the future in playwriting. The production of John Osborne's Look Back in Anger in 1956 ushered in a new generation of playwrights, directors, actors and designers who together established the Court as the first theatre in London that prioritised the work of contemporary playwrights. Among them were Arnold Wesker, Ann Jellicoe, Edward Bond, John Arden, Christopher Hampton and David Storey. New plays were programmed alongside classics, and the company was from its earliest days committed to producing the best new international plays, including those of Ionesco, Genet and Beckett.

In 1969 the Royal Court opened the first second space in a British theatre; the Jerwood Theatre Upstairs has been a site for radical experimentation and has introduced audiences to some of the most influential new voices of the last 40 years, including Wole Soyinka, Caryl Churchill, David Hare, Howard Brenton, Howard Barker, Peter Gill, Martin Crimp, Sam Shepard and Jim Cartwright. Many outstanding young playwrights have established their careers here; among them Joe Penhall, Sarah Kane, Roy Williams, Rebecca Prichard, Mark Ravenhill, Martin McDonagh, Conor McPherson, Simon Stephens and debbie tucker green.

The Royal Court's Artistic Programme is only partially about the work seen on its stages. Many of its resources, and indeed the roots of the organisation, are devoted to the discovery and nurturing of new writers and the development of new plays. The Royal Court is in the business of asking questions about the world we live in and about what a play itself can be. The theatre's aim is to support both new and established writers in exploring new territory.

The Royal Court has a rich and productive infrastructure for the discovery and development of playwrights:

photo: Stephen Cummiiskey

International Programme

Since 1992 the Royal Court has initiated and developed lasting relationships with international playwrights and theatre practitioners. Creative dialogue is ongoing with theatre practitioners from many countries, including Brazil, Cuba, France, Germany, India, Mexico, Nigeria, Palestine, Russia, Spain and Syria. Many of the world's most promising and exciting playwrights have presented their plays on the stages of the Royal Court, among them Marcos Barbosa, Roland Schimmelpfennig, Marius von Mayenburg, Vassily Sigarev, the Presnyakov brothers and David Gieselmann. All of these influential projects are generously supported by the Genesis Foundation and the British Council.

The Young Writers Programme

The Young Writers Programme seeks to open up theatre to the most exciting and diverse range of new voices around today, encouraging and inspiring young writers to use theatre as a means of exploring their world, and helping them to flourish as artists. Week-long intensive playwriting projects for the 13-16 and 16-19 age groups are run during school holidays and each season playwriting groups for the 18-25 age group are led by resident playwriting tutor Leo Butler.

Rough Cuts

The Royal Court's plays have frequently challenged the artistic, social and political orthodoxy of the day, pushing back the boundaries of what is acceptable or possible. That tradition of experiment and provocation is intensified in the Rough Cuts seasons of experimental collaborations between playwrights and other artists, which are presented as raw and immediate works-in-progress in the Jerwood Theatre Upstairs.

The Royal Court's long and successful history of innovation has been built by generations of gifted and imaginative individuals. For information on the many exciting ways you can help support the theatre, please contact the Development Department on 020 7565 5079.

INTERNATIONAL PLAYWRIGHTS AT THE ROYAL COURT

Since 1992 the Royal Court has placed a renewed emphasis on the development of international work and a creative dialogue now exists with theatre practitioners all over the world including Brazil, Cuba, France, Germany, India, Mexico, Nigeria, Palestine, Romania, Russia, Spain and Syria, and with writers from seven countries from the Near East and North Africa region. All of these development projects are supported by either the British Council or the Genesis Foundation.

The Royal Court has produced new International plays through this programme since 1997. Recent work includes On Insomnia and Midnight by Edgar Chías (Mexico), My Name is Rachel Corrie, Amid the Clouds by Amir Reza Koohestani (Iran), Way to Heaven by Juan Mayorga (Spain), At the Table and Almost Nothing by Marcos Barbosa (Brazil), Plasticine, Black Milk and Ladybird by Vassily Sigarev (Russia) and Terrorism by the Presnyakov Brothers (Russia). All of these productions have been supported by the Genesis Foundation.

Kebab is presented as part of the International Playwrights Season, A Genesis Project, produced by the Royal Court's International Department:

Associate Director **Elyse Dodgson**
International Administrator **Chris James**
International Assistant **William Drew**

The Genesis Foundation supports the Royal Court's International Playwrights Programme. To find and develop the next generation of professional playwrights, Genesis funds workshops in diverse countries as well as residencies at the Royal Court. The Foundation's involvement extends to productions and rehearsed readings. Genesis helps the Royal Court offer a springboard for young writers to greater public and critical attention. For more information, please visit www.genesisfoundation.org.uk

Kebab is a co-production between the Royal Court Theatre, Ulster Bank Dublin Theatre Festival and Pentabus Theatre Company with additional support from the Romanian Cultural Institute, London.

New Romanian Playwrights at the Royal Court

The Royal Court began its collaboration with emerging Romanian writers in 1998 when we ran a series of workshops for young playwrights from all parts of the country in Târgu Mures. Since 1998, seven Romanian playwrights and one director have attended the Royal Court International Residency including Gianina Carbunariu (2004) director Cristian Popescu (1998), and writers Alina Nelega-Cadariu (1999), Andreea Valean (2001), Theo Herghelegiu (2003), Stefan Peca (2005) Veronica Ion (2006), and Maria Manolescu (2007).

In 2002 a commissioned short play, Where the Smoke's Going, by Andreea Valean was performed as part of the International Playwrights Season.

In November 2006 a new group of 13 writers began working with playwright Rebecca Prichard and director Orla O'Loughlin as part of a new long term initiative between the Royal Court, the British Council and the Uniter Foundation. This work was supported by the Genesis Foundation.

INTERNATIONAL SEASON

Jerwood Theatre Upstairs

International Playwrights: A Genesis Project

8 – 24 November
FREE OUTGOING
by **Anupama Chandrasekhar**

30 November – 21 December
FAMILY PLAYS:
a double bill

THE GOOD FAMILY
by **Joakim Pirinen**
translated by **Gregory Motton**

THE KHOMENKO FAMILY CHRONICLES
by **Natalia Vorozhbit**
translated by **Sasha Dugdale**

ULSTER BANK DUBLIN THEATRE FESTIVAL 1957 – 2007

The Ulster Bank Dublin Theatre Festival celebrates its 50th Anniversary in 2007. Established in 1957, it is the oldest dedicated theatre festival in Europe, and one of the last surviving English language theatre festivals in the world. The Festival is unique in Ireland in its ability to stage major international theatre of scale, and has hosted productions by many of the world's most highly regarded artists and companies including Peter Brook, Robert Lepage, The Maly Theatre, Romeo Castellucci, Complicite and Steppenwolf Theatre Company. Throughout its history the Festival has consistently premiered work by the leading Irish companies including the Abbey Theatre, the Gate Theatre, Druid and Rough Magic.

The Festival has a long and illustrious association with the very best of new Irish writing. Works by Seamus Heaney, Roddy Doyle, Brian Friel, Neil Jordan, Hugh Leonard, Frank McGuinness and Tom Murphy have all premiered during the Festival. In recent years a whole new generation of Irish writers have presented work on the Festival programme, including Conor McPherson, Martin MacDonagh, Enda Walsh and Marina Carr.

For the past number of years, the Ulster Bank Dublin Theatre Festival has undertaken the role of supporting and developing major new pieces of work that, without the Festival's support, could not have come to fruition. Most recently the Festival has co-produced Giselle (2003) and The Bull (2005) with Michael Keegan Dolan's Fabulous Beast Dance Theatre. The final part of Fabulous Beast's Midlands Trilogy, James son of James, will be presented in 2007 in a co-production with Ulster Bank Dublin Theatre Festival, barbicanbite08 and Dance Touring Partnership.

The Ulster Bank Dublin Theatre Festival is delighted to be co-producing a new work with the Royal Court for the first time, and hopes that this relationship will continue to nurture and support Irish writers, and writers writing about Ireland, for many years to come.

50th Anniversary Ulster Bank Dublin Theatre Festival: September 27th - October 14th 2007
What Will You Think?
www.dublintheatrefestival.com

PENTABUS THEATRE COMPANY

Pentabus Theatre Company occupies a unique position in British touring theatre. Based in Shropshire, one of the most rural parts of the UK Pentabus has existed for over 30 years. Developing new writing has always been at the heart of the Pentabus' work and it has established itself as one of the country's leading   producing companies, commissioning and touring new plays nationally and internationally. The company also maintains a strong local presence bringing its work to places where very little opportunity exists to see or take part in live arts events.

In the past five years Pentabus has broken the mould for small-scale touring companies, creating work that has achieved acclaim at a national level: its output can only be categorised by its high quality, variety of approach and scale of ambition. The company is free to go where its artistic vision takes it.

Work is often inspired by the company's location in one of the most beautiful parts of the country and is always a product of its commitment to collaboration with the artists, venues and organisations that share that vision. This way the company establishes a close relationship with writers and artists, nurturing their ideas through workshops and residencies.

Recent productions include: Silent Engine by Julian Garner (Fringe First Award); Precious Bane adapted by Bryony Lavery and performed outdoors at stately homes across the country ('if you only see one piece of theatre this summer see this!' Guardian); Strawberry Fields, Alecky Blythe's verbatim exploration of the use and abuse of migrant labour in Herefordshire and White Open Spaces, a collection of single person dramas, each a reaction to Trevor Phillip's statement that a 'passive apartheid' exists in the English countryside. In 2006 the play ran at the Pleasance in Edinburgh, The Soho Theatre and Writers Centre, Riksteatern in Stockholm and was broadcast on BBC Radio 4. It was nominated for a South Bank Show Award earlier this year.

www.pentabus.co.uk

PROGRAMME SUPPORTERS

The Royal Court (English Stage Company Ltd) receives its principal funding from Arts Council England, London. It is also supported financially by a wide range of private companies, charitable and public bodies, and earns the remainder of its income from the box office and its own trading activities.

The Genesis Foundation supports the Royal Court's work with International Playwrights.

The Jerwood Charity supports new plays by new playwrights through the Jerwood New Playwrights series.

The Artistic Director's Chair is supported by a lead grant from The Peter Jay Sharp Foundation, contributing to the activities of the Artistic Director's office. Over the past ten years the BBC has supported the Gerald Chapman Fund for directors.

American Friends of the Royal Court are primarily focused on raising funds to enable the theatre to produce new work by emerging American writers. AFRCT has also supported the participation of young artists in the Royal Court's acclaimed International Residency. Contact: 001-212-946-5724.

FOR THE ROYAL COURT

The first major UK revival of two ground-breaking plays first performed at the Royal Court in the 1960s.

Performed in Repertoire

21 September – 15 December

rhinoceros
by Eugène Ionesco

In a new translation by **Martin Crimp**
Direction **Dominic Cooke**
Design **Anthony Ward**
Lighting design **Johanna Town**
Sound design **Ian Dickinson**

Sponsored by **Coutts & Co**

1 November – 15 December

the arsonists
by Max Frisch

In a new translation by **Alistair Beaton**
Direction **Ramin Gray**
Design **Anthony Ward**
Lighting design **Johanna Town**
Sound design **Ian Dickinson**

500 tickets
£5 for 25s
and under*

020 7565 5000
www.royalcourttheatre.com
Royal Court Theatre, Sloane Square, London SW1

ARTS COUNCIL ENGLAND

KEBAB

Gianina Cărbunariu

KEBAB

Translated by Philip Osment

OBERON BOOKS
LONDON

First published in 2007 by Oberon Books Ltd
521 Caledonian Road, London N7 9RH
Tel: 020 7607 3637 / Fax: 020 7607 3629
email: info@oberonbooks.com
www.oberonbooks.com

Cover image by Michelle Thompson

ISBN: 1 84002 809 2 / 978-1-84002-809-6

Printed in Great Britain by Antony Rowe Ltd, Chippenham.

Characters

MĂDĂLINA

BOGDAN

VOICU

Note

Although the actors speak in English throughout, the characters are speaking in 'Romanian'. When dialogue appears in bold, the characters themselves are speaking in 'English'.

SCENE 1

On an aeroplane.

ANNOUNCEMENT: **...and the captain and the crew would like to welcome you on board this Tarom flight from Bucharest to Dublin and wish you a pleasant journey.**

BOGDAN is in the window seat but avoiding looking out.

MĂDĂLINA is looking over his shoulder not particularly concerned about whether she's disturbing him. She crosses herself several times.

MĂDĂLINA: That's cool. God, that's so cool!

BOGDAN: Do you want to change seats?

MĂDĂLINA: No I can see like this.

Short pause.

Your first time?

BOGDAN: In Ireland?

MĂDĂLINA: No, on a plane. Like first time on a plane.

BOGDAN: Kind of.

MĂDĂLINA: Me too. Really cool, isn't it?

BOGDAN: Yeah, cool. Cool

MĂDĂLINA: (*Looking at BOGDAN's camera.*) That's really cool. Shall I take your photo?

BOGDAN: I'm not photogenic.

MĂDĂLINA: Shit. I come out really well in photos.

BOGDAN: I haven't got enough battery.

Short pause. BOGDAN sees MĂDĂLINA looking fixedly at the sandwich in front of him.

MĂDĂLINA: They don't give you much to eat, do they?

BOGDAN: You can have it.

MĂDĂLINA: No, I've got to be careful I don't put on weight.

Short pause. She takes the sandwich and eats it hungrily.

Not feeling very well, are you?

BOGDAN: What do you mean?

MĂDĂLINA: You look a bit shit.

BOGDAN: I'm very sensitive to some smells.

MĂDĂLINA: Yeah?

BOGDAN: Yeah. Stinks of perfume in here. It's making me feel sick.

MĂDĂLINA: That's me. I tried on about 27 at the airport. What else is there to do for two hours?

BOGDAN: Right.

MĂDĂLINA: But I didn't find anything I liked.

Short pause.

I'll get myself something really nice once I'm in Ireland. Voicu – my boyfriend – told me I'll be able to buy as many as I like.

BOGDAN: Right.

MĂDĂLINA: I'm moving there, see. Going to live with Voicu, my boyfriend. He's Irish.

BOGDAN: He's got a Romanian name.

MĂDĂLINA: Yeah, just his name's Romanian, but like, he's actually been Irish for over a year.

BOGDAN: Right.

MĂDĂLINA: He's over there making money. He's working in a bar.

BOGDAN: Right

MĂDĂLINA: He's promised he's going to help me find a job in, like, a shop selling really cool clothes and shit.

BOGDAN: Great

MĂDĂLINA: I just have to learn English.

Short pause.

English is really important. You have to be able to understand people and be, like, understood.

BOGDAN: Right.

MĂDĂLINA: So what's your English like? You get by?

BOGDAN: I'm going to be doing an MA in Visual Arts. I'll be studying in English.

MĂDĂLINA: Oh, you're a student.

BOGDAN: Yes. But really advanced.

MĂDĂLINA: Really? So what you going to be studying?

BOGDAN: Visual Arts.

MĂDĂLINA: Cool. Like…what exactly?

BOGDAN: Photography, film, stuff like that, visual stuff.

MĂDĂLINA: And can you earn money doing that sort of thing?

BOGDAN: I'm going over there to learn, not to make money.

MĂDĂLINA: But you wanna, like, stay there don't you?

BOGDAN: That's sort of the idea.

MĂDĂLINA: There's no way I'm ever going back. No way.

BOGDAN: Right.

MĂDĂLINA: If you work hard and stuff, they really appreciate you over there. That's what Voicu, my boyfriend, told me. It's different

BOGDAN: Yeah.

MĂDĂLINA: I was really lucky meeting Voicu. If it hadn't been for him I wouldn't have left. It's harder on your own, isn't it?

BOGDAN: Yeah.

Pause.

MĂDĂLINA: Hey listen, if you *do* want to make a bit of money, I could talk to him – he already knows loads of people over there.

BOGDAN: If he knows that many people over there…we'll probably bump into each other one way or another.

MĂDĂLINA: Fair enough. But if you do run into Voicu tell him you know Mădălina. Actually…Maddy! That's my Irish name. Apparently they don't have Mădălina over there.

BOGDAN: No, not really.

Short pause.

MĂDĂLINA: So listen, what's your name?

BOGDAN: Bogdan.

MĂDĂLINA: You could be Bobby or something!

BOGDAN: I think Bogdan's fine.

MĂDĂLINA: Yeah right. Names aren't going to be a problem. Being good at what you do, working like crazy and making money – that's the thing.

BOGDAN: Right.

MĂDĂLINA: You have to prove how great you are – like the greatest!

BOGDAN turns right round to the window. MĂDĂLINA makes herself more comfortable in her seat.

(*Whispering in his ear.*) Listen, you sure you haven't got enough battery left for a photo?

SCENE 2

A cheap bedsit in Dublin. Maddy is looking at a 50 Euro banknote. VOICU is massaging her feet.

MĂDĂLINA: BCE, ECB, EZB, EKT, EKP, two zero zero two…what the fuck is all that supposed to be? Buildings, bridges…stars, one star, two stars, three stars, four stars, five stars, six stars, seven stars, eight stars, nine stars, ten stars, eleven stars, twelve stars! Look, that's Europe… We are here, next to the stars and a month ago I was…over here where the map finishes. You see that? They haven't got old farts on their money. Looks cool this, without the old farts.

Short pause.

Today it was like that fat cow was looking at me weird, you know? Like she was trying to catch me out or something. Really pisses me off when people stare at me. So I went to the bog and stuck my finger up my nose and got a massive bogey. Rolled it into a big ball and then split it up into smaller and smaller ones. Like fifteen really small balls. Then I went back and waited for her to take an order. Stuck them in the meat – they looked like little peppercorns. It was great. Much better than spitting.

VOICU tickles her till she lets go of the banknote. He folds it and puts it in his pocket.

VOICU: You smell of onions.

MĂDĂLINA: I'll go and have a shower.

VOICU: I was in a pub opposite your kebab shop today. I saw you…

MĂDĂLINA: Seriously?

VOICU: Yes, I was having a beer watching you… You've got a really great body – supple like a gymnast, give me a hard-on right away. I was thinking – what if I went in there right now and lifted your skirt and gave you a good seeing to right there on the counter – in front of all those tossers chewing and chewing and chewing on their shitty kebabs? More mayonnaise, sir? Then these two guys came in the pub – two Romanians…

MĂDĂLINA: I missed you too.

VOICU: Close your eyes a minute.

He takes out a mobile with a video screen.

MĂDĂLINA: You get me something?

He takes a photo. MĂDĂLINA opens her eyes when she hears the sound

VOICU: High tech. Brand new.

MĂDĂLINA: You got me a mobile?!!!

VOICU: (*Taking another photo of her.*) Polyphonic ringtones, games, organizer, radio, shit hot video – it's got everything.

MĂDĂLINA: How much did you pay for it?

VOICU: Those guys I met in the pub today… We had a beer together…they gave it to me.

MĂDĂLINA: Is it stolen?

VOICU: You think I'm crazy enough to give 400 Euro for a phone?

MĂDĂLINA: Let me see what it's got on it.

He gives her the mobile.

VOICU: I'll give you my old one so you've got one too –

MĂDĂLINA: I thought it was for me…

VOICU: I'll get you one exactly the same once we've got our hands on some cash. Right now we need money for food, for clothes and for the rent. If we don't pay the rent in three days' time, we'll be sleeping on the streets.

Short pause.

So, from tomorrow you won't be going to the kebab shop any more. I've found you something else. Ten times better paid.

MĂDĂLINA: Seriously?

VOICU: Seriously. It's all set up.

MĂDĂLINA: Cool! Will I have to stand up all day?

VOICU: It's something completely different.

MĂDĂLINA: Something, like, really cool, yeah?

VOICU: You won't be on your feet all day and you won't stink of kebabs any more – that's for definite.

MĂDĂLINA: And you think I'll be able to do it?

VOICU: You bet.

MĂDĂLINA: When do I start?

VOICU: In about an hour.

MĂDĂLINA: In an hour?

VOICU: We have to move fast. You have your shower and chill out. I'll make you a nice strong coffee with lots of sugar.

SCENE 3

A mobile rings.

MĂDĂLINA: Yeah?

VOICU: Hello? Where the fuck are you? Why didn't you answer your phone? I thought something had happened to you... Well? Go on! Where are you?

MĂDĂLINA: Don't know.

VOICU: What do you mean you don't know?

MĂDĂLINA: They threw me out the car.

VOICU: Those fucking bastards. Did they hurt you?

MĂDĂLINA: They threw me out the car...think I sprained my ankle when I fell.

VOICU: Did you get lippy with them?

MĂDĂLINA: You never told me they were off their heads, they were high as kites!

VOICU: All you had to do was spend an hour with them. Your attitude is losing us money for fuck's sake! How much have we made this week?

MĂDĂLINA: You try spending an hour with the total fuckwits you keep coming up with.

VOICU: Mădalina, how much money have we made this week? Just answer me that. Then I'll come and pick you up.

MĂDĂLINA: Well if you'd hadn't tried to be so clever finding rich punters in town!

VOICU: That's what it said in the paper: 400 an hour! That's how much the Polish and Lithuanian girls get paid.

MĂDĂLINA: Those guys are professionals... What's with getting paid afterwards? Who ever heard of that?

VOICU: You think I didn't try? We're not the only ones on the market. Tell me where you are.

MĂDĂLINA: Nowhere.

VOICU: What you mean, nowhere?

MĂDĂLINA: I have no fucking idea. How should I know where I am?

VOICU: Well have a look round and tell me what you can see.

MĂDĂLINA: I can see... I can see some cars.

VOICU: Oh well done! You must be able to see a building or something...

MĂDĂLINA: There isn't any building. There's just a motorway. I'm by a motorway.

VOICU: So you're not in the city.

Pause.

See if you can see a road-sign with something on it – a number, anything –

MĂDĂLINA: I can't see a thing, it's pitch dark.

VOICU: Well get up and have a look round.

MĂDĂLINA: My ankle's killing me!

VOICU: Take a deep breath. Deep breath! You'll soon feel better. Just breathe with me. And one, and two, and three... Deep breaths.

Actually only VOICU is breathing. MĂDĂLINA is trying to get up.

Better? Tell me you're feeling better.

MĂDĂLINA: Never felt better in my life.

VOICU: You getting up?

MĂDĂLINA: Yes.

VOICU: You up?

MĂDĂLINA: Yes.

VOICU: Bollocks...! Come on, deep breaths. Deep deep breaths. Hey! Are we breathing or not?

MĂDĂLINA doesn't answer him. She tries to get up.

Mădălina, we breathing or what?

MĂDĂLINA: Not breathing.

VOICU: Fine. Not breathing. Whatever you want. Fuck! Cunt! My battery's going. How far are you from the road?

MĂDĂLINA: I'm on the verge. Right on the verge.

VOICU: Great. On the verge is great. Now stick your hand up, stick up your hand – someone's bound to stop…

MĂDĂLINA: What am I supposed to tell them if they do?

VOICU: Nothing. Don't tell them who you are, don't tell them what you do, just give the address and ask them very nicely to take you home.

MĂDĂLINA: Home where?

VOICU: My battery's going. **Portland Row, number 40.**

MĂDĂLINA: Say it again.

VOICU: Repeat after me: **Please.**

MĂDĂLINA: **Please.**

VOICU: **Take me home.**

MĂDĂLINA: **Take me home.**

VOICU: **Dublin Portland Row.**

MĂDĂLINA: **Dublin Portland Row.**

VOICU: **Number 40.** Say it again from the start! And look, make sure you don't go stopping a police car because then we're really fucked. You know what police cars look like, don't you!

His battery goes.

Oh cunt!

SCENE 4

Men's toilet in a Dublin pub. BOGDAN is peeing at one of the urinals. VOICU comes to pee in the next urinal. They speak in very basic (accented) English. All the same BOGDAN's English is much more advanced that VOICU's.

VOICU: **Guinness, right?**

BOGDAN: **Right.**

VOICU: **Guinness is the best.**

BOGDAN: **Right.**

VOICU: **Sorry, Irish?**

BOGDAN: **No. Italian.**

VOICU: **Pizza, pizza is the best also.**

BOGDAN: **Right.**

VOICU: **Pizza, Guinness and sex! It's the best, man.**

BOGDAN: **Sure.**

He pulls up his zip.

VOICU: **But sex is the best.**

He puts his hand on BOGDAN's shoulder wanting to seem friendly but BOGDAN steps back.

No, don't worry, not with me, with a woman... Pamela Anderson, big tit? Jennifur Lopez, big ass? Tina Turner, big hair? I have everything for you very cheap!

BOGDAN: **No, mate, I'm not interested.**

He starts to go. VOICU takes his mobile out of his pocket.

VOICU: **Wait a little! Look here! I show Jennifur for you.**

BOGDAN: **Really mate, I have to go, I have friends, they are waiting for me...**

VOICU: **Two second! Photo is for free, you can see Jennifur. Look!**

He shows BOGDAN some photos on the phone.

Beautiful tit, beautiful smile...

BOGDAN: **Look, I don't have much money...**

VOICU: **Very cheap! 60 normal fuck, 40 blow job.**

BOGDAN: **Blow job...**

VOICU: **Blow job is the best! 40 Euro for Jennifur!**

BOGDAN: **10 for Jennifur.**

VOICU: **35 for Jennifur.**

BOGDAN: **15 for Jennifur.**

VOICU: **30 for Jennifur.**

BOGDAN: **No more than 20 for Jennifur.**

VOICU: **Okay you can take Jennifur!**

BOGDAN: **I'll be waiting for her in a white car, near McDonald's.**

VOICU: **No, no McDonald's, here in the toilet.**

BOGDAN: **In the toilet?**

VOICU: **Yes, in the toilet. Toilet is the best!**

BOGDAN: **No, mate, I don't like toilets...**

VOICU: **You don't like toilets...** You fucking cunt!

BOGDAN: **Okay, forget it...**

Slightly panicked BOGDAN starts to go again.

VOICU: (*Stopping him.*) **Five minutes. McDonald's five minutes.**

BOGDAN: **Okay, five minutes.**

He starts to go.

VOICU: **Money?**

BOGDAN: (*Panicked.*) **Money...after.**

VOICU: **Money now! Money now, man!**

BOGDAN: **No, money after...**

VOICU: **Okay, see you!**

BOGDAN: **Wait. I give you half now, half after!**

VOICU: **No fuckin' tricks!**

BOGDAN: **No fuckin' tricks!**

VOICU: **So we have a deal?**

BOGDAN: **Yeah, we have a deal.**

They slap hands. Blackout.

SCENE 5

In the car – sound of brakes. Both their faces are lit up every so often by the lights of passing cars.

Short pause.

BOGDAN: Stupid fucking twat!

MĂDĂLINA: Not only are you a shit driver, but you're Romanian as well. Don't I know you from somewhere?

BOGDAN: Don't think so. I don't usually…

MĂDĂLINA: I didn't say I'd sucked you off before, I just said I know you from somewhere.

BOGDAN: We don't exactly move in the same circles…

MĂDĂLINA: We met on the plane two months ago.

BOGDAN: Don't remember.

Pause.

Weren't you going to work in a shop or something…

MĂDĂLINA: It wasn't that easy.

BOGDAN: Anyway…you've changed, you look much…

MĂDĂLINA: Taller. By five centimetres. I'm fucking growing.

BOGDAN: Yes, you've got…yes.

MĂDĂLINA: Haven't got a girlfriend over here then?

BOGDAN: How do you know? Of course I have… I'm seeing this girl, she's…anyway we're going out, it's wicked…saw her only last night and we… You know, it's none of your business!

MĂDĂLINA: Alright then…

She tries to undo his trousers.

BOGDAN: What about you…what you been up to?

MĂDĂLINA: This and that. You have to do something, don't you?

BOGDAN: I've been really busy. At college.

MĂDĂLINA: Good for you.

BOGDAN: It's really cool.

MĂDĂLINA: Good for you, you got it made.

BOGDAN: Everything's cool and I haven't got a single idea.

MĂDĂLINA: Shit.

BOGDAN: All the other students came with ideas, and subjects and proposals. I'm the only one who hasn't proposed anything yet. Tomorrow's the deadline. But I haven't got any sort of project.

MĂDĂLINA: Shit.

BOGDAN: Deep shit. I haven't got a single idea, not a single crappy idea.

MĂDĂLINA: Shit.

BOGDAN: How am I supposed to feel inspired if I still don't understand fuck-all about where I've landed? I still can't figure out this place. I've got a block, yeah? At home I used to have ten good ideas a day. Here I don't even get a crap one in a week. One of the other guys has lent me his car, see. So that I can get my head round left being right and right being left. It's not easy, not at all easy. People are okay, you know, they help you out, they lend you their cars, the shop assistants smile at you, the beer's good – what can I say? – the whole system works. It's just me – I don't work. I thought if I started to do just, like, the basic things, like drive a car, pay by card, read their newspapers, smile more often myself, chill out more...chill out a lot more.

He scratches his head. He catches MĂDĂLINA looking at him.

My hair's falling out.

MĂDĂLINA: Shit.

BOGDAN: I don't mean it's falling out like...one or two hairs. I mean by the fucking handful. I wake up in the morning and my pillow's black, covered in hairs. Hundreds of them. I keep treating it but it still falls out. Just keeps falling out. Every morning I count how many there are. I set my alarm earlier so that I've got time to count them…it even made me late for a class one time. I'm going to be getting up at bloody four in the morning just so I've got time to count my hairs.

MĂDĂLINA: Why don't you shave your head?

BOGDAN: Why? So I won't even know if I've gone bald. Look, at the moment there are 70 hairs on my shoulders. Count them!

MĂDĂLINA: You might have one or two…

BOGDAN: You've no idea how much my scalp itches. It makes me want to scratch it with a knife. I pull off bits of skin big as this. It just comes off with the hair on it I tell myself to chill out, chill out, all you have to do is chill out a bit. It just gets worse. Itch, itch, scratch, scratch.

Pause.

What am I supposed to do tomorrow at college? What shall I do? Tear all my hair out in front of them.?

MĂDĂLINA: I'm really sorry.

BOGDAN: Shut the fuck up!

He starts to cry, resting his head on the steering wheel.

MĂDĂLINA lights a cigarette. Smokes and looks at her watch.

MĂDĂLINA: You can carry on crying for another five minutes. We've got plenty of time.

BOGDAN lifts his head from the steering wheel and leans back.

BOGDAN: Go on then. Go on, do it.

MĂDĂLINA bends down to his flies.

A few minutes later.

I've got my camera. Battery's charged.

Pause.

I could take your photo if you like.

Pause.

MĂDĂLINA: I've got more photos than I need, thanks.

Pause.

I suppose I could give you my gran's address and you could send it home for me. It would make her happy.

BOGDAN: You want me to say anything?

SCENE 6

Horror cartoons – Gymnastics: Our girls always take Gold.

TRAINING IS VERY IMPORTANT

MĂDĂLINA: We're living in a civilised country. Yep. Nothing like Romania. Look at the toilets for example, toilets are a sign of civilisation. No, nothing like Romania. And I've changed too since I've been here. Now I shave myself all over. Hair's a sign that you're uncivilised. Voicu told me that of course. So now I shave all over. To begin with I was a bit sensitive. Not any more. Slowly my skin got used to it, it's tough as old boots now. What doesn't kill you, makes you stronger.

TEAM GOLD

Romanian girls really are the best – it's not just me saying that, ask anyone. Voicu thought this way was the most efficient and least dangerous: ten minutes, cash upfront.

Of course he was right. So I had to apply myself, perfect my skills, improve my performance, till I was the best. All my punters, Easterners, Westerners, all sorts, they were all very satisfied: **'Fuckin' good blow job! Where are you from?' 'Romania,'** that's what I told them.

COMPULSORY ROUTINES

Anal. That was the hardest. But there's a lot of demand for it, what can you do? Voicu trained me: 'If you can take it from me, then you can take it from anyone.' I've got a tattoo here, it says **MADE IN ROMANIA** – 'In case you forget where you're from,' – not that I would forget. And on my arse I've got **WELCOME TO IRELAND**. 'If it hurts think about something else.'

I think and I think and I think – what the fuck should
I think about?…a shop full of perfumes, I pick out
something French-sounding – whatever that may be – fuck
knows!

A HIGHLY COMPETITIVE FIELD

'We're losing out because of all these perverts!' that's
what Voicu says, 'Everywhere you look there's queers and
paedophiles, it's the end of the world, the Apocalypse,
that's what it is, Sodom and Gomorrah. I should go and
buy myself a few hens, a cow and a sheep.' I'd quite
like that, to be honest. We'd be, like, farmers, Ireland's
supposed to be a very good place for rearing animals. I
wouldn't mind having a farm like that. And if we had, say,
ten cows and each of them had at least five punters a night
like me…we'd be made, we'd be rich over night. We'd be
filthy rich!

FLOOR EXERCISE

I think I could have had a career as a dancer. I danced
for a punter once. We didn't have any music so I sang a
Jennifer Lopez song. But that twat just didn't get it. He kept
on with: **ROMANIAN, ROMANIAN**, he wanted me to sing
and dance in Romanian. **I AM NOT NADIA COMANECI**,
I told him, I'm not Nadia Comaneci you know and if you
want Folklore go and live in Romania. See how wonderful
it is.

ON THE PODIUM

Home? This isn't my home, but then home's not home
either. Because home is worse than anywhere that's not
home. Never going back home. Never going back. No.

SCENE 7

BOGDAN is filming MĂDĂLINA.

MĂDĂLINA: Who's going to see this?

BOGDAN: The other students, the lecturers – if it comes out
well, loads of people will.

MĂDĂLINA: You stupid? What if one of them, like, goes to the police?

BOGDAN: Relax, I'm not filming your face.

MĂDĂLINA: What sort of film hasn't got any faces in it?

BOGDAN: It's conceptual.

MĂDĂLINA: Whatever! I just don't want to be deported.

BOGDAN: I give you my word.

MĂDĂLINA: Screw your word. When a Romanian says he gives me his word, it makes me want to take a shit. It's automatic.

Short pause.

What am I going to get out of all this?

BOGDAN: If the film comes out how I want it to…

MĂDĂLINA: What's in it for me?

BOGDAN: It'll be easier for me to get a job and I'll be able to help you find something.

MĂDĂLINA: If Voicu finds out he'll cut me up into little pieces and throw me in the Liffey. He'll do the same to you.

BOGDAN: He'll only find out if you tell him.

VOICU enters.

VOICU: Buona sera.

BOGDAN: Fuck!

VOICU: Comment ça va? Ça va bien?

BOGDAN: **I can explain everything.**

VOICU: **Of course, of course…** But let's use Romanian, because we speak the same language, don't we?

BOGDAN: Yeah, I think we do.

VOICU: Right, take a seat, make yourself at home.

They all three sit on the sofa with BOGDAN in the middle. They're silent for a few seconds. BOGDAN's bag is right in front of VOICU. VOICU picks it up and opens it.

May I?

BOGDAN: No! I mean, yes, of course. But I haven't got anything valuable in there, you know. Money or…

MĂDĂLINA: He's hasn't – he's just a student…he hasn't…

VOICU: What you take me for? Think I want to rob our client, our employer? I'm just a bit curious, that's all.

VOICU takes out a wallet and opens it. He finds BOGDAN's student ID card and passport.

Bogdan Ionescu. **Student, post-gra-du-ated studies. Visual Arts.** Uhhuh. And what exactly are you studying at this place?

BOGDAN: Visual Arts.

VOICU: Put simply for us, that means…?

BOGDAN: Photos, videos…

MĂDĂLINA: Like, visual stuff.

VOICU: Do they still have places?

BOGDAN: I don't know, I could find out if you like…

VOICU: Please do. Looks interesting. I'm really into technology. And I'd love to make these sorts of films.

BOGDAN: Look, let me explain: I'm making a film for an exam –

VOICU: Wicked.

BOGDAN: Pardon?

VOICU: Nice photo. Like it. You'd think you were Italian. Your hair suits you like that. (*To MĂDĂLINA.*) Look, suits him, doesn't it?

MĂDĂLINA: Come on, leave him alone.

VOICU: Who's talking to you? So why are you interfering? Get in the kitchen and bring us two beers. (*To BOGDAN.*) You'll have a beer with me, won't you?

BOGDAN: Yeah, I suppose so.

BOGDAN starts to scratch his head. VOICU examines his camera, fascinated, as if it's a new toy, pushing buttons randomly. BOGDAN scratches his head more and more furiously.

VOICU: That's the water. It's really bad here. Well, until you get used to it. Know what you should do? You should use an egg. You take an egg, you take it, crack it, separate it, I mean just take the yolk, and use it on your head. Nice. Then you wait five minutes and...tara! You have to rinse really well. That's what I did and look – no problem!

BOGDAN: I'll try it.

VOICU: You should. And afterwards?

BOGDAN: After what?

VOICU: After your exam. You going back to Romania?

BOGDAN: Don't think so.

VOICU: Good man! If you've got talent, why waste it?

BOGDAN: That's what I was thinking.

VOICU: So you got anything set up over here?

BOGDAN: Not yet...but I'm hoping to get something soon.

MĂDĂLINA enters with the beers.

VOICU: See? We're getting on really well. (*To BOGDAN.*) Cheers, man.

BOGDAN: Cheers.

VOICU: I've been thinking lately, I've been looking around. Wherever I look, man, all I see is crime.

BOGDAN: Right.

VOICU: You can't trust anyone. Someone says they're a serious client and then what do they do?

BOGDAN: Just let me explain...the idea is that I make a film...

VOICU: ...they give the girl a pill, they beat her up, throw her out the car, but I think Maddy's already told you all that...

BOGDAN: Briefly.

VOICU: Anyway you know the score. Just one setback after another, man. One after another.

BOGDAN: Yes, that's the way it can go.

VOICU: So I started thinking, I started having a look through the newspapers, 'cos I don't know if Maddy told you –

BOGDAN: Just very briefly. But I'd just like to explain so you know exactly what it is I'm trying to –

VOICU: Look man, are you listening to what I'm saying here? What's your fucking hurry? So, I don't know if Maddy told you but unlike her, I'm not bad at English. And I read, I read a lot, you have keep yourself well-informed, don't you?

BOGDAN: Yes, I suppose you do.

VOICU: 'Course you're a student, so you know all this. Right, so do you know what I've been reading lately? You won't believe it, man! What have I been reading?

BOGDAN: Don't know. What?

VOICU: Internet sites.

BOGDAN: Right.

VOICU: Picture this, right, I'm here at home, I turn on the computer, get Maddy, do stuff with her and other people sit and gawp at us. What's more they pay for it. I've heard that you can make a mint from it.

BOGDAN: It's no big deal, you just need a computer and –

VOICU: 'Course you're a student, you know all this. Personally I think it's something it might be worth investing in.

BOGDAN: I suppose so...

VOICU: Thing is, I need someone to give me hand, at least to start with, until I'd got the hang of it.

BOGDAN: Right.

VOICU: There you are, then. This is your lucky day.

BOGDAN: (*Uncertainly.*) Really...?

VOICU: I've got a job for you.

BOGDAN: A what?

VOICU: A job. In a one hundred per cent Romanian enterprise. Me, you and Maddy.

BOGDAN: And what would my job sort of entail?

VOICU: Look, if I'm going to invest in this then I want it to be a bit more artistic. Some of the sites I've seen – I've been doing my research – you know? – and some of them are pathetic, not worth looking at. But you're an expert, you could be a sort of, a sort of…what's his face…like a sort of Spielberg.

BOGDAN: A sort of director.

VOICU: Exactly.

(*To MĂDĂLINA*.) I told you we'd speak the same language.

BOGDAN: And what would I get out of this 'enterprise'?

VOICU: I'll let you have Maddy. For free. You can sit and listen to all her crap to your heart's content. And money of course, if we make money, then I'll let you have money as well. It's bloody expensive living here, as you know. What you say?

BOGDAN: I've got a laptop,

Pause.

I'll bring it round… But you'll need to invest in a webcam as well, we'll need one if –

VOICU: **So, we have a deal?**

BOGDAN: **Yes, we have a deal.**

VOICU takes his hand.

VOICU: I'll see you out.

BOGDAN goes. VOICU returns immediately and sits on the sofa. He takes MĂDĂLINA in his arms.

Well done! It went better than I expected.

MĂDĂLINA: I want you to give me back my passport. Now.

VOICU: You want it right this minute?

MĂDĂLINA: Wasn't that the deal? If I brought him here, you'd give me back my passport.

VOICU: I wanted to give you a surprise for Christmas, but I suppose I'd better tell you now otherwise you'll be driving me up the wall... I sold it. To some bloke, a Moldavian. I got a good price. If I'd waited a month I'd have been able to ask for twice as much but I thought you'd really need a winter-coat or –

MĂDĂLINA: Why didn't you sell yours?

VOICU: Because he was offering more for yours than mine, that's why. It was fake anyway...

MĂDĂLINA: You're fucking mad!

VOICU: So here's me slogging away to make you a porn star, buying you furs and stuff, and you're still not happy. What else do I have to do? – just to hear you say you're happy. I'd just like to hear you say it once – I am happy!

MĂDĂLINA: I am happy.

VOICU: Don't believe you.

MĂDĂLINA: I am *verrrrrry* happy

VOICU: Don't mess me about! What are you?

MĂDĂLINA: I am very happy.

SCENE 8

The same room. The laptop and the camera are set up in front of the sofa. BOGDAN and Mădalina sit on the sofa BOGDAN is filming her. VOICU is sitting on the floor in front of the sofa looking through an Irish newspaper.

MĂDĂLINA: **I am, you are, he are –**

BOGDAN: **He is.**

MĂDĂLINA: **He is, we are, you are, they are.**

BOGDAN: Well done. Now make a sentence.

MĂDĂLINA: **We are.**

BOGDAN: Go on, make a longer sentence.

MĂDĂLINA: Well what should I say?

BOGDAN: I don't know…we are at home, go on.

MĂDĂLINA: **We are home.**

BOGDAN: **At home. We are at home.**

MĂDĂLINA: **We are at home.**

BOGDAN: Now say something about yourself.

MĂDĂLINA: **I am… I am… I am sexy.** Is that right?

BOGDAN: 'S correct. Now say something about me.

MĂDĂLINA: **You are…you are…** How do you say wicked over here?

BOGDAN: **Wicked…nice…**

MĂDĂLINA: **You are wicked nice.**

BOGDAN: Now say something about Voicu.

MĂDĂLINA: What do you say when, like, someone's not from here?

BOGDAN: **Stranger, foreigner.**

MĂDĂLINA: **Voicu are…**

BOGDAN: **Voicu is.**

MĂDĂLINA: **Voicu is…**

VOICU: **I am here!** And that's the end of the lesson. Enough! I've had it up to here, it's given me a fucking headache. Jesus, for three days all I've heard is **I am** and **He is**…

MĂDĂLINA: That's not true. I've learnt **I have**, **I do**, **I want** and **To be**. That's the hardest.

BOGDAN: Tomorrow I'll teach you the future tense, that's the easiest.

VOICU: Don't bother – she won't be needing it.

MĂDĂLINA: You never know.

She repeats.

I am, you are, he is…we are, you are, they are…

There's a beep from the laptop. BOGDAN and VOICU react. BOGDAN goes to the laptop.

VOICU: That's enough pissing about. Our public awaits!!

MĂDĂLINA: **I am sexy! I am sexy!**

Another beep from the computer. VOICU slaps her.

You are wicked nice.

Insistent beep. VOICU slaps her again.

You are stranger foreigner.

VOICU strikes her again. Her nose bleeds. MĂDĂLINA covers her face with her hands.

VOICU: Go to the bathroom and clean yourself up. Now!

BOGDAN: (*Sitting down with the camera behind the laptop.*) Let her stay like that. (*To MĂDĂLINA.*) Take your hands away from your face. Look at me.

SCENE 9

They're sitting on the floor surrounded by McDonald's bags and beers.

VOICU: What an Easter! All these shitty e-numbers – call it food? – it's packaged fucking shit. I've put on ten kilos since I've been here.

MĂDĂLINA: Me too, I've put on weight as well.

VOICU: You have to be careful, it's dangerous at your age, you'll start ballooning out and you won't stop. No more hamburgers, no more beers, look at the belly you've got on you.

BOGDAN: I think that's a lot sexier.

MĂDĂLINA sits on BOGDAN's lap and kisses him on the cheek.

Anyway voluptuous women are more marketable!

VOICU: Voluptuous women are ones with big tits not ones with two buttons on a ginormous belly.

MĂDĂLINA: They'll get bigger.

VOICU: Get bigger? In the seven months you've been here they look like they've shrunk. Maybe it's the Irish air.

MĂDĂLINA: Or the water. If his hair's falling out…

BOGDAN: It's stopped falling out lately.

VOICU: You used the egg yolk.

BOGDAN: No. It just stopped.

VOICU: I told you, to start with it's hard, but you get used to it in the end.

BOGDAN: Yeah, although this is a really stressful time for me.

VOICU: Oh come on, you've got another month and a half before the deadline, loads of time.

Short pause.

BOGDAN: Know what I'd like to eat now? Ciorbă de burtă.

VOICU: Now you're talking. People here haven't got a clue. With garlic sauce, cream and pickled chillies! My Mum's sarmale are out of this world, and her bean soup with bacon and onion, and her cozonac, and pasca and drob... Listen, if it doesn't work out with the website, we'll set up a traditional Romanian restaurant, we'll call it Dracula or Transylvania or something to bring in punters –

MĂDĂLINA: I know how to make fried egg and chips, rice pudding and onion omelette.

VOICU: Leave the cooking to me, Bogdan can do our publicity, right? And we'll dress you up in a nice costume, something traditional, 'cos they're mad about folk customs and stuff and you can be like a waitress or something.

Short pause.

BOGDAN: I love the cozonac my Mum makes at Easter. She gets up at the crack of dawn and kneads the dough and leaves it to rise, and it rises and rises until it comes out of the bowl, she layers it with loads of walnuts and sultanas and Turkish Delight, then she sticks it in the oven and in ten minutes you can smell it all over the house, in the whole block, it's like – the smell of it fills up the whole estate.

VOICU: At home I'm stuffed the whole time, here I'm always starving. I never feel full, I never manage to say, that's it,

I've eaten and I'm full up. Good job you can get drunk on their beer. I mean it'd be really shit if you were dying of hunger all the time and sober into the bargain.

BOGDAN: I miss the smells. Most of all I miss the smell of cozonac with milk. I could get full just on the smell of –

VOICU and MĂDĂLINA begin to laugh. VOICU begins to sniff at MĂDĂLINA's wrists.

VOICU: (*To BOGDAN.*) Smell this!

MĂDĂLINA: Voicu says I smell of cozonac and milk.

VOICU: Go on, around her wrists and her neck…

BOGDAN smells.

MĂDĂLINA: I'd like to smell of French perfume not of cozonac with milk.

VOICU: Don't be daft, any woman can smell of French perfume, but I don't think many could boast that they smell of cozonac with milk…

MĂDĂLINA: Stop it, that tickles! Stop it.

VOICU bites her neck, BOGDAN her calf. Blackout.

SCENE 10

HORROR CARTOONS – FAIRYSTORIES FROM CHILDHOOD

MĂDĂLINA: I'm not Maddy any more. No, I'm not Maddy any more. I'm little Red Riding Hood – running like mad through the forest.

BOGDAN: I'm not Bogdan any more. No, I'm not Bogdan any more. I'm the boy who cries wolf and makes the townsfolk think he's coming to eat them up.

VOICU: I'm not Voicu any more. No, I'm not Voicu any more. I'm the eldest of the three little billy-goats – the naughty one who opens the door to the wolf.

MĂDĂLINA: I'm running, running through the big dark forest…

BOGDAN: I'm shouting and shouting and shouting to make all the foolish townsfolk come running...

MĂDĂLINA: I've got lots of goodies here. Can you smell?

BOGDAN: And I'm laughing and laughing and laughing at the foolish townsfolk.

MĂDĂLINA: Can you smell all the goodies I've got?

VOICU: I'm hiding behind the door...holding my breath, hiding behind the door.

MĂDĂLINA: Can you smell? I've got lots of goodies here.

BOGDAN: I'm just a little child, the naughtiest child of all, just a little child...

MĂDĂLINA: Lots and lots of goodies.

BOGDAN: I'm a child, the naughtiest child of all, just a little child...

VOICU: I'm a tender little billy goat, a very tender little billy goat...

BOGDAN: Just a little child...

VOICU: Very very tender...

MĂDĂLINA: I've got lots and lots of goodies...

BOGDAN: Just a little child...

VOICU: Very very tender...

MĂDĂLINA: Lots and lots of goodies..

BOGDAN: Just a little child...

VOICU: Very very tender...come on, come and eat me up...

MĂDĂLINA: Come and eat me up..

BOGDAN: Come and eat me up...

VOICU: Come and eat me up!

MĂDĂLINA: Come and eat me up!

BOGDAN: Come and eat me up!

VOICU: Come and eat me up!

MĂDĂLINA: Come and eat me up!

BOGDAN: Come on, come and eat me up.

All three of them take a breath.

That's right!

MĂDĂLINA: That's right.

VOICU: That's right.

SCENE 11

The three of them are sleeping together, MĂDĂLINA is in the middle. They have to squeeze up because there's so little space. MĂDĂLINA tries to find a comfortable position.

VOICU: What's wrong with you?

MĂDĂLINA: I can't sleep.

VOICU: Nor can I, but I'm trying not to disturb anyone else who might be tired and want to –

BOGDAN: I can't get to sleep either, don't know what the hell's wrong with me.

Pause.

MĂDĂLINA: I keep thinking...maybe it wasn't such a good idea to come here. I mean to Ireland –

BOGDAN: Why?

MĂDĂLINA: America's supposed to be better. Its easier in America, that's why they call it 'the land of opportunity'.

BOGDAN: Everywhere's hard.

MĂDĂLINA: Yes, but over there it's worth the struggle. Look, maybe you'll do well in your course but you're never going to be, like, a Spielberg, because you're not in Hollywood.

BOGDAN: I don't want to be Spielberg. I'm doing other things.

MĂDĂLINA: Okay. I wouldn't mind being Jennifer Lopez, but that's not going to happen here. I won't even be Madonna.

VOICU: No, you won't. So shut up and go to sleep.

Pause.

MĂDĂLINA: I keep thinking…what have I actually done since I been here? I mean compared to what I was doing at home. Nothing. I get beaten up every day –

BOGDAN: Back there you get beaten up for nothing. Here you make money from it.

MĂDĂLINA: But what can I do with it? They haven't even got bloody Disneyland here. We could have gone on Sundays. I'm sick of staying in all the time.

VOICU: I'll give you Disneyland if you don't shut up. Go to sleep.

Pause.

MĂDĂLINA: (*Whispering to BOGDAN.*) I was thinking… I was thinking I wouldn't like to die here.

BOGDAN: Why not?

MĂDĂLINA: 'Cos if you don't have money here, they burn you and throw away the ashes. It's shit, being burnt. I'd smell like a kebab, an' all.

BOGDAN: Who told you that load of bollocks?

VOICU: I did. To get her motivated. If you're not motivated you don't survive, end of story.

BOGDAN: Doesn't matter how hard it is here, it's still a lot better.

MĂDĂLINA: America would have been best.

VOICU: That's it. I've just about had it! What's with all this America shit? It's fine here! Whether I'm here or in America, what I need is to be able to go back home and feel fucking great. Back there everyone calls me Irish and gives so much to drink that I only come round on the plane. Last time my Mum put half a pig in my bag without me knowing. When I got to check-in the guy asked me, 'What's this, sir?' 'What do you think it is?' I said, ' A souvenir!'

Short pause.

If I have to stay here and struggle so that I can feel good at home for three days a year then I'll stay here and struggle. Let's stop talking shit and go to sleep.

Pause.

It's got very cold all of a sudden, man.

He takes MĂDĂLINA in his arms.

BOGDAN huddles up to the other two and puts his arms around MĂDĂLINA too.

BOGDAN: Bloody cold.

Pause. They remain pressed together.

MĂDĂLINA: The sun shines all the time in California.

SCENE 12

BOGDAN: **Yeah, yeah, I know where this is... Okay. I'll be there in one hour. See you!**

He rings off.

VOICU: Where you going?

BOGDAN: Party. Have to get changed.

MĂDĂLINA: Cool! Can we come?

BOGDAN: I don't know, I'd better ask...it's just a small gathering – other students from the MA.

MĂDĂLINA: That'll be really cool. We'll get to know your Irish friends.

BOGDAN: They're not all Irish.

MĂDĂLINA: Even better.

BOGDAN: I don't know if I can bring anyone.

MĂDĂLINA: Phone and ask then.

BOGDAN: Parties here aren't like ones at home...we'll be talking about college...you'll get bored.

VOICU: He's right. What are we gonna do there?

MĂDĂLINA: If we get bored we'll just push off.

VOICU: Free drinks?

BOGDAN: Yeah, I guess…although I don't know. It may not be.

VOICU: Phone and ask then.

(*To MĂDĂLINA.*) Have you got anything to wear?

MĂDĂLINA: I'll find something…give me five minutes.

She goes quickly to get dressed.

BOGDAN takes out his phone and makes a call.

BOGDAN: Actually I don't know if I still want to go… Same old discussions, same old people, I see them all at college anyway, so… No, there's no point going really.

VOICU: What do you mean? That's not very nice after they've invited you.

BOGDAN ends his call.

BOGDAN: Mmmm, no answer.

VOICU: Well try again.

BOGDAN tries to call again. MĂDĂLINA appears in a short red dress. VOICU starts laughing. BOGDAN hangs up.

MĂDĂLINA: How do I look?

VOICU: Well, fuck me if you don't look like Little Red Riding Hood. After she's been shagged by the wolf and the bear and the rabbit and the hunter all at once.

BOGDAN: You look really nice…except we're not going. They're not answering the phone and I don't really feel like it…

MĂDĂLINA: I feel like it. I've got dressed up now!

BOGDAN: Why don't we get some drinks in and stay home?

MĂDĂLINA: How am I supposed to learn to speak better English if I'm just stuck at home with you two? I want to meet people too, you know!

VOICU: You've met quite enough people. What if somebody there recognises you? How's Bogdan gonna feel?

BOGDAN: No, it's not that. We'll go another time, I promise.

MĂDĂLINA: But I want to go now!

BOGDAN: Now…now isn't a good time.

MĂDĂLINA: Don't I look nice or what?

BOGDAN: No, you look very nice…

MĂDĂLINA: I don't believe you.

BOGDAN: You're really pretty and that dress really suits you, it's just that…

Beep from the computer.

VOICU: It's just that it's not for tarts or kebab shop girls. When the man says NO, you just don't get it, do you? So go and take that crap off or I'll rip it off you and you won't like that one little bit.

BOGDAN approaches MĂDĂLINA and begins to undress her, talking to her at the same time.

BOGDAN: You look really really nice… It's just they're not answering the phone, what can I do? We can't just turn up, that's not civilised, but next time you can put on the same clothes and we'll go together, it will be really wicked, you wait and see. After I finish the project everyone will want to meet you, you'll be guest of honour, just wait and see.

Blackout.

SCENE 13

VOICU and BOGDAN are sitting on the floor sharing a cigarette. MĂDĂLINA is lying on the sofa.

BOGDAN: Fuck me, it's still raining.

VOICU: Yeah.

BOGDAN: Fed up with it.

VOICU: You're too sensitive. I've got used to it.

BOGDAN: What day's it today?

VOICU: Why?

BOGDAN: Have to go to the editing suite. Still got work to do.

Pause.

Someone from college has put in a good word for me with an advertising company. I should get an interview.

VOICU: Great. That means you'll be able to stay legally

BOGDAN: Yes. But the thing is I won't be able to do whatever I like any more. I won't have time for my own stuff.

VOICU: But you'll be able to carry on working with us on the website.

BOGDAN: Of course, if I've got time

VOICU: What do you mean if you've got time? We're friends, we'll stay together whatever happens.

Short pause.

I'm really pleased, you know, that you've completely moved in with us. That's the hard thing: setting yourself up with a family – but like, a real family, with like brothers, parents, sisters, cousins, second cousins, uncles, aunts, friends and relations. So you can go visiting and have get-togethers with lots of food and drink and fights…

BOGDAN: I don't know if that's what I miss most

VOICU: Depends on your temperament. I'm a family man.

BOGDAN: Yeah.

VOICU: My hand hurts.

BOGDAN: You should be more careful.

VOICU: I got carried away.

Pause.

Did you put that T shirt in to soak?

BOGDAN: Yes. I hope it comes out, I got it here, it's designer.

VOICU: Did you rinse it in cold water like I said?

BOGDAN: Wonder what time it is.

VOICU: Late. It'll be getting light soon.

BOGDAN: If it's Friday I have to go to college.

VOICU: Stay here – probably Sunday already.

BOGDAN: It's depressing staying here doing nothing.

VOICU: You're too sensitive. Maddy never complains. If you ask her nicely she'll wash your T shirt tomorrow. Maddy's an example of someone who's got balls. Here, watch: Maddy!

MĂDĂLINA lets out a little sound in her sleep.

See, she can hear me, she recognises me, she knows I'm here beside her, waiting for her to wake up, she knows I'll take care of her. Go on, you call her.

BOGDAN takes a drag on the cigarette.

Call her.

BOGDAN: Maddy!

VOICU: Call her again.

BOGDAN: Mădălina!

VOICU: See, she doesn't recognise you as easily. Listen you really think all this stuff is going to bring us in more money?

BOGDAN: Yes, of course, the hard stuff is more expensive. Besides there's my project, we had a deal.

VOICU: But couldn't we do some stuff…some special effects? With cherry syrup and chocolate – it's supposed to look the same colour as… And it tastes nice…so Maddy would like that too. I wouldn't like anything to happen to her, you know…

BOGDAN: If you'd been more careful nothing would have fucking happened.

VOICU: I couldn't be more careful. It's all right for you, moving round us with that fucking camera in your hand.

BOGDAN: I thought you wanted to make money…

VOICU: Okay, man, but all the same couldn't we do some special effects? You said you were an expert! What the fuck do they teach you there?

BOGDAN: Okay. I'll have a think.

Pause.

It's still fucking raining.

VOICU: You're too sensitive, man. I told you, you're just too sensitive.

BOGDAN: Right.

While they're talking MĂDĂLINA puts her hand to her mouth and tries to get up, she starts to throw up. BOGDAN quickly gets the camera and begins to film her.

VOICU: What's wrong? What the hell is wrong? I told you not to eat all that shit!

(*To BOGDAN.*) And what he hell are you doing?

He feels sick too and runs to the bathroom.

BOGDAN: Just let me do my job.

SCENE 14

HORROR CARTOONS – ABRAKEBABRA

All three are laughing in their sleep.

MĂDĂLINA: Abracadabra. I'm not Maddy any more and I'm not Red Riding Hood.

BOGDAN: Abracadabra. I'm not Bogdan any more and I'm not the boy who cried wolf.

VOICU: Abracadabra. I'm not Voicu any more and I'm not the eldest little billy goat.

MĂDĂLINA: Now I'm kebab meat.

BOGDAN: Fresh kebab meat.

VOICU: Sliced kebab meat.

MĂDĂLINA: Grilled kebab meat.

BOGDAN: Abra-ke-babra…

VOICU: Abra…kebabra?

MĂDĂLINA: Abra…abrakebabra…

BOGDAN: Abrakebabra!

VOICU: I don't know why…

BOGDAN: No, I don't know why –

MĂDĂLINA: I don't know, I don't know why…

VOICU: I don't know why, but every night…

BOGDAN: No, no, I don't know why…

MĂDĂLINA: I don't know why, but every night I dream that I'm a doner kebab.

Blackout.

SCENE 15

In the flat. BOGDAN is dressed differently than usual – much more smartly. MĂDĂLINA films him.

MĂDĂLINA: Veeery sexy!

BOGDAN: It went quite well. Better than I expected.

MĂDĂLINA: Great! Did they like me?

BOGDAN: They liked the idea…the way I filmed it…the special effects.

MĂDĂLINA: What special effects?

BOGDAN: That's the point. Yeah, it was good.

MĂDĂLINA: Great. And the job interview?

BOGDAN: Got it.

MĂDĂLINA: Seriously? Are they going to pay you well?

BOGDAN: Enough for me to rent somewhere and live.

MĂDĂLINA: Great. I'm pregnant.

Pause.

BOGDAN: What did Voicu say?

MĂDĂLINA: Haven't told him, it's none of his business.

BOGDAN: How do you know it's not his?

MĂDĂLINA: He's just been hitting me lately.

BOGDAN: When did you find out?

MĂDĂLINA: Two months ago. I didn't want to stress you out. I've thought it all through: we move in together, have the baby, you find me some sort of work... You promised.

BOGDAN: Hang on, let's get this straight...

MĂDĂLINA: I thought we already had. We passed the course, didn't we? We got a job? Because we work so well together.

BOGDAN: And Voicu?

MĂDĂLINA: Don't care. I love you.

BOGDAN: I have to sort out my job, find a flat... I'll... I'll ring you in a few days' time.

MĂDĂLINA: No. I'm coming with you. I'm all set.

BOGDAN: You can't come to the halls with me.

MĂDĂLINA: Why not?

BOGDAN: For fucking fuck's sake, you can't come now – just get that into your head! You can't wait a couple of days?

MĂDĂLINA: No. And watch your fucking language – I'm pregnant – I'm not supposed to get upset.

Sound of a door, BOGDAN and MĂDĂLINA look at each other. VOICU enters.

VOICU: Hiya! Where've you been keeping yourself? I've been trying to track you down but your phone's been off.

BOGDAN: Been busy.

VOICU: (*Hugging him.*) Congratulations! Well done!

BOGDAN: How did you know?

VOICU: I met your room-mate. Great guy.

BOGDAN: You've been to my room?

VOICU: You've been staying in *our* room haven't you? So, you've got yourself sorted. (*To MĂDĂLINA.*) I told you he'd get himself sorted and then he'd come round here, he's not going to just disappear into thin air. Right I'm going to go and get us some beers and we'll get pissed! I told you everything would be all right. Didn't I tell you?

BOGDAN: Yeah, everything will be great, only I won't have as much time for the website. I mean I won't really have any time.

VOICU: You'll manage somehow. We can work nights.

BOGDAN: But that's the thing, I'm going to be…you gotta understand, I'm just starting and so…

VOICU: Hang on, I thought we were friends…

BOGDAN: We *are* friends. We'll stay friends. I'll come and visit.

VOICU: You wanna move out? Why do you want to do that? I thought we got on, I thought we were like a family.

BOGDAN: We can't carry on living together like this.

VOICU: Why not?

BOGDAN: Because.

Short pause.

VOICU: We had a deal.

BOGDAN: Temporarily.

VOICU: I helped you, you help me. To the end. That was the deal.

BOGDAN: I'm sure you'll manage on your own.

MĂDĂLINA: I can't work any more either. I'm pregnant.

Short pause.

We're both leaving.

VOICU: Seriously?

MĂDĂLINA: Yes.

BOGDAN: (*At the same time.*) No.

VOICU: Make your minds up.

BOGDAN: I've really gotta go. I'll take my stuff and…

VOICU: No. First I want to know what's going on.

MĂDĂLINA: (*To BOGDAN.*) Tell him we have made up our
minds.

Pause.

Tell him we decided we're going to move in together and
have the baby and you're going to find me a good job.

BOGDAN: You're nothing to do with me, get that into your
head. I want to live normally. A normal life.

Pause.

VOICU: (*To MĂDĂLINA.*) It's no big deal, I'll bring up the kid.
We'll bring him up together. We'll give him some sort
of Irish name, Jim, Jerry, something like that, send him
to school to learn English…and then we'll send him to
America, to fucking Hollywood.

MĂDĂLINA: I'm going with him.

Pause.

You're a loser. (*To BOGDAN.*) I'll go and get my bags. You
get your stuff and in five minutes we'll be out of here.

She goes.

There's a beep from the computer.

VOICU: When did you say you start work?

BOGDAN: Week's time.

VOICU: Bravo. It'll take you a few months to get used to it.
And then one day, when you have just got used to it, and
you're there drinking your coffee behind your nice clean
desk with all your plans spread out in front of you and all
your felt tip pens, an under-age girl with a great bulging
belly appears at the door to your office and she comes and
introduces herself to all your Irish colleagues who couldn't
give shit about you anyway, she comes and introduces
herself and says, 'I'm his wife, I'm fifteen years old, I've

sucked off half of Dublin, we're going to have a baby together and we're very happy!' Just try and visualise that, 'cos that's your job, visualising things, isn't it? Have you visualised it?

Pause.

But if we come to an agreement that you're going to put up so much a month then everything will be hunky-dory for all concerned. We're not going to fleece you but you have to chip in – you know how expensive it is to live here. We have to stay friends and help each other out.

There's another beep from the computer.

MĂDĂLINA enters.

MĂDĂLINA: I'm ready. (*To BOGDAN.*) Let's go then. Come and give me a hand – these are heavy.

VOICU takes the camera and starts filming while BOGDAN speaks.

BOGDAN: You two are nothing to do with me. Is that so difficult to understand?

Pause.

The end. Give me the camera! Give me the camera.

BOGDAN stretches out his hand to take the camera. VOICU takes it and pulls him onto the floor. He kicks him in the stomach.

VOICU: I don't like violence. I don't like having to treat a friend like this – I don't understand you. I treated you so well, we shared the same woman.

There's another beep from the computer. VOICU looks at MĂDĂLINA.

You gone deaf? Come on, get on with it.

The beeps become more and more insistent.

(*To BOGDAN.*) Get a move on, we're losing money.

BOGDAN: I can't…

VOICU: Course you can. How do you think I managed? And I want it to be for real. You were right. The hard stuff costs more.

They look at each other. VOICU gets ready to film. The beeps become more and more insistent.

Blackout.

SCENE 16

HORROR CARTOONS – NIGHT FLIGHT

BOGDAN: I took the window seat
In the belly of the White Flying Wolf.

VOICU: I took the aisle seat
In the belly of the White Flying Wolf.

MĂDĂLINA: I took the seat in the middle
In the belly of the White Flying Wolf

ALL: We're going home
In Business Class!

Can we have a double scotch, please?

BOGDAN: Ladies and Gentlemen
This is the white flying wolf
This is your Captain speaking

VOICU: We'll be flying by night
A round trip flight.

MADDY: Home from home
Without stopover
Non-stop! We wish you pleasant dreams.

ALL: Can we have another double scotch, please?

BOGDAN: May I have your attention please!
We're experiencing some turbulence
A nightmare patch of turbulence.

VOICU: Please fasten your safety belts
And try to go to sleep.

MĂDĂLINA: We'd like to wish you warmly
    the sweetest of dreams.

ALL: Can we have another double scotch, please?

BOGDAN: May I have your attention, please?
    I'm afraid we're losing altitude
    We seem to be in free-fall and taking a dive.

VOICU: Owing to a regrettable error
    The aircraft has been overloaded
    We have to lose weight as quickly as we can.

MĂDĂLINA: And what's more, someone's having a very bad
    dream.

ALL: Can we have another double scotch, please?

BOGDAN: May I have your attention please?
    Please put on the life jackets situated beneath your seats.

VOICU: Oxygen masks will fall
    From the panel above your heads.

MĂDĂLINA: And we'd ask you to locate
    The nearest exit from your dream.

ALL: Can we have another double scotch, please?

BOGDAN: May I have your attention please?
    Someone on the aircraft is having a very bad dream.

VOICU: Someone is putting everyone's life at risk.

MĂDĂLINA: Someone is ignoring all the safety instructions.

ALL: Can we have another Scotch please? Make it a triple!

BOGDAN: May I have your attention please,
    We're running out of whiskey
    There are only two more measures
    And I'm sorry to announce that there's no more ice at all.

VOICU: Someone has to jump.

MĂDĂLINA: Someone has to jump

BOGDAN: Someone has to jump.

ALL: There's no time to lose.

BOGDAN: Eeny meeny miny mo
Catch a spider by the toe
If he wriggles let him go
Eeny meeny miny mo

BOGDAN points at MĂDĂLINA.

MĂDĂLINA: Eeny meeny miny mo
Catch a spider by the toe
If he wriggles let him go
Eeny meeny miny mo

MĂDĂLINA points at VOICU.

VOICU: Eeny meeny miny mo
Catch a spider by the toe
If he wriggles let him go
Eeny meeny miny mo

VOICU points at BOGDAN.

ALL: One last time!
Eeeny meeny miny mo
Catch a spider by the toe
If he wriggles let him go
Eeeny meeny miny mo

Each of them points to him/herself.

VOICU: May I have your
attention please?

MĂDĂLINA: This is your
Captain speaking.

BOGDAN: May I have your
attention please?

VOICU: This is your
Captain speaking. May
I have your attention
please?

MĂDĂLINA: May I have
your attention please?

BOGDAN: This is your
Captain speaking.

SCENE 17

Another flat in Dublin, which looks much better, much brighter than the other one. BOGDAN is working on the computer.

VOICU: The living room is the most important room in the house. Civilised people spend all their time in the living room. Television, beer, pizza...all mod cons.

Short pause.

Well, in the end they get bored stupid, that's why civilised people also go to work. We hardly see each other for more than half an hour a day.

Short pause.

And when you *do* finally get home, you don't want to do anything. I go mad on my own.

Pause.

Will you be working late again this week?

Pause.

Doesn't matter, I'll wait. I cleaned the tiles in the kitchen and the bathroom, did you see?

Pause.

Out of boredom.

Short pause.

Listen, maybe I should start cooking, homemade stuff like my Mum, what do you think?

Pause.

I know, tomorrow I'll make sarmale. But you'll have to leave me some money 'cos it's bloody expensive to make sarmale here.

Pause.

It's no problem, I like cooking, you know?

Pause.

Let me have it now, you'll forget later.

I went out for a while today, you know? Walked around Grafton Street, went into the camera centre. You won't believe what I saw. Know what I saw? Polaroid cameras. Look!

He takes out a Polaroid camera and shows it to BOGDAN.

It was really cheap. And I thought how cool it would be if I had one so I could take photos and send them home, my family would love that, I've never sent them a photo from here…they'd be able to see how well we're doing. The shit thing was that I didn't have any money to get a film

– they're quite expensive so I thought maybe you could give me some...

BOGDAN: For fuck's sake...

Short pause.

We'll get some films with my next wages.

Pause.

VOICU: Think I could do with a drink. You going to go or shall I? It's okay, I'll go... You want anything else?

Starts to go, then returns.

I forgot to tell you. I got tickets for the match on Sunday.

Pause.

The Ireland-Romania match.

Pause.

The National Game!

Pause.

So, fuck your presentation. We have to go and support the lads.

We have a deal?

BOGDAN: **Yeah, we have a deal.**

They slap hands.

VOICU: We're going to blow them away, just like at home: allez, allez, allez, allez, allez!

BOGDAN joins in with VOICU, they both start shouting like at a stadium with closed fists:

BOTH: Allez! Allez! Allez! Allez! Allez!

The End.